This book is inspired by and
dedicated to
future and armchair travelers.
Many, many thanks to
family and friends
who support and inspire me.

*Bernadette Meier*

ISBN: 9-780692-183847

First printing 2018
Bernadette Meier
www.artbybernadette.com
artbybernadette@gmail.com

# If you went on a safari to Zambia, in Africa,

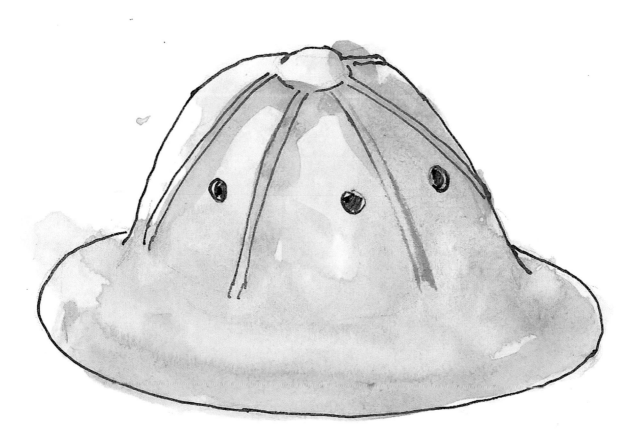

# Here's what you might see...

Written and illustrated by Bernadette Meier

A very

Splashy

elephant,

Or an elephant
PARADE

crossing a river!

A family

of monkeys.

Just one hippo
floating on his own,

Or a
bunch
of hippos
playing!

A zebra

striped in

**black**

and

Lots and lots of

BIRDS!

Kingfisher

Bee eater

Blue helmeted
Guinea

A very

giraffe

An acacia tree

Or a lazy lion

After all this,
you may see
them forever
in your dreams!

## About the artist...

Bernadette Meier is an ink and watercolor artist living in Upstate New York.
A lifelong artist, she loves walking, traveling, and creating art.
When any of those are combined, it puts her in 'the flow'.

Bernadette likes working on site best, but often takes photos to work from later. She mostly works in watercolor sketchbooks, with nearly two dozen filled so far.
Her art travel kit consists of a micron and fountain pens, pencil, eraser, brushes and a watercolor tin.

See Bernadette's latest work here:
www.artbybernadette.com
Or email her directly: (She would love to hear from you!)
artbybernadette@gmail.com

Made in the USA
Middletown, DE
09 July 2019